Little Pebble™

Holidays Around the World

Chinese New Year

by Lisa J. Amstutz

CAPSTONE PRESS
a capstone imprint

Little Pebble is published by Capstone Press,
1710 Roe Crest Drive, North Mankato, Minnesota 56003
www.mycapstone.com

Library of Congress Cataloging-in-Publication Data
Library of Congress Cataloging-in-Publication data is available on the Library
of Congress website.
ISBN 978-1-5157-4851-9 (library binding)
ISBN 978-1-5157-4857-1 (paperback)
ISBN 978-1-5157-4875-5 (eBook PDF)
Summary: Explains how people prepare for and celebrate the holiday of
Chinese New Year.

Editorial Credits
Jill Kalz, editor; Julie Peters, designer; Pam Mitsakos, media researcher;
Steve Walker, production specialist

Photo Credits
Getty Images: MIXA, 9, View Stock, 11; iStockphoto: FangXiaNuo, 6, IS_ImageSource,
15; Shutterstock: 123Nelson, 21, asharkyu, cover, freelion, 7, iBird, 5, macbrianmun,
10, maoyunping, 1, passion artist, design element, Sofiaworld, 3 bottom left, Tan Kian
Khoon, 20 bottom right, Toa55, back cover, topten22photo, 19; Superstock: Blue Jean
Images, 17, Neil Farrin / robertharding, 13

Printed and bound in China.
PO7884LEOS17

Table of Contents

Happy New Year!

Pop! Boom!

Fireworks fill the sky.

It is Chinese New Year!

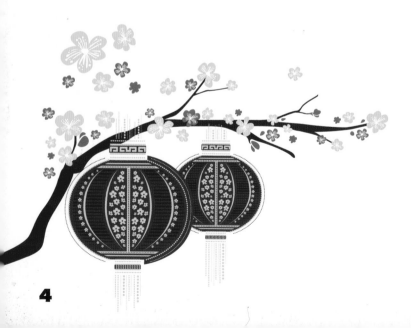

This holiday is in January or February. It lasts many days.

Let's Get Ready

People clean their homes.

They sweep out bad luck.

People hang red scrolls.

Red is a lucky color.

Many people shop for gifts.
They buy flowers. They get
new clothes.

Time for a Party

It is New Year's Eve!

Families gather.

They eat a big meal.

The next day, kids get red envelopes. Money is inside. Friends visit. They bring wishes for good luck.

The holiday ends with
a parade. Lanterns glow.
People eat sweets.
They beat drums.

Dancers dress up as lions. A dragon runs by. People cheer. Happy New Year!

Glossary

envelope—a flat, folded paper

fireworks—rockets that make loud noises and colorful lights when they explode

lantern—a container for a light

parade—a line of people, bands, and floats that travels through a town for a special event

scroll—a roll of paper with writing on it

Read More

Carr, Aaron. *Chinese New Year.* Let's Celebrate American Holidays. New York: AV2 by Weigl, 2014.

Heinrichs, Ann. *Chinese New Year.* Mankato, Minn.: Child's World, 2013.

Pettiford, Rebecca. *Chinese New Year.* Holidays. Minneapolis: Jump!, Inc., 2016.

Internet Sites

FactHound offers a safe, fun way to find Internet sites related to this book. All of the sites on FactHound have been researched by our staff.

Here's all you do:
Visit *www.facthound.com*
Type in this code: 9781515748519

Check out projects, games and lots more at
www.capstonekids.com

Critical Thinking Using the Common Core

1. How do people get ready for Chinese New Year? (Key Ideas and Details)

2. Name three red things that may be seen during Chinese New Year. (Key Ideas and Details)

Index